HOW TO BE FUNNY, INTERESTING, AND MAKE PEOPLE LIKE YOU

LEARN HOW TO MAKE FRIENDS

MICHAEL MURPHY

CONTENTS

Introduction   v

1. Friendship   1
2. Make a Good First Impression   4
3. Be Interestingly Funny   7
4. Be Memorable   9
5. Learn To Listen   11
6. Your Body Language   13
7. Do Your Research   16
8. Social Media   18
9. Get a Hobby   20
10. Comedic Delivery   23
11. Fashion, Panache and Comedy   25

Afterword   27

INTRODUCTION

This book teaches you how to make a good impression and keep it. To be more specific, the impression you want to give is to be "interesting" and "have the ability to make people laugh".

Think of yourself as a performer. You want to get the attention of the audience. You want to be memorable, and give off a good vibe. You are the person who is perceived as fun and interesting.

If you want to be funny and interesting, you need to know yourself.

What is it about you that people will find interesting?

Let's begin!

1

FRIENDSHIP

Friendship is a kind of relationship based on a mutual affection between two or more individuals. Its foundation is more on inter-personal bond among people rather than by simple association.

Friendships come in many different forms, shapes and sizes. You can be friends with anybody you want. In fact, there are times when you become friends with people you least expected you will be friends with.

Although there a lot of ways to make friends, it is best to start making friends with people to whom you can share common interests with.

So before further discussing how to start making friends, here are simple steps in starting a friendship that you should know about:

STEP 1: Meet People

Since friendship is a relationship to be shared by two or more people, the first step that you should do is to go out and meet as many people as you can. You can do this by following what interests you. Don't hesitate to join social clubs, sports teams or even religious organizations. You can also meet people by attending community gatherings or events that involve social interaction. Try to join activities that meet regularly because it will mean that you'll be meeting the same people over and over again, thus increasing the chances of making new friends. This step may take time for you to establish a connection or rapport with possible friends, so be sure to actively participate in all the things the group will be doing for you to get to know them better and vice-versa.

Step 2: Start a Conversation

For you to show people that you can make a good friend, the next step you need to do is to start a friendly conversation. During the conversation, it is important that you show that you are a good listener and that you are genuinely interested with the people you are talking to. You can do this by continuously making eye contact while talking. Also, be sure that you give relevant comments and ask the right questions. Lastly, don't forget to smile all the time.

Step 3: Do Stuff Together

The last step in starting a friendship can be done only after a connection has been made. Once you have established a bond, you should now elevate the friendship to the next level. How? Encourage your future friends to do stuff together outside your comfort zone. But be sure that the things that you and your friends will be doing are things that you all like to do. You can't force what you like to your friends so it is important that you first ask them what kind of stuff they want to do.

2

MAKE A GOOD FIRST IMPRESSION

When making friends, one of the most important things to do is to make a very good impression of your self. And when you say good impression, it literally and figuratively means being able to "impress" people in a "good" way. For people to like you and actually want you to be included in their circle of friends, you should prove them that you are indeed friend-material.

But making a good impression is easier said than done because you wouldn't want to overdo impressing people. The best way to go is to act as natural as you are and just be yourself all the time.

Here are some things that can help you in making a good first impression to your friends:

1. **Always be on time.** If you are to meet somebody for the first time, it is a must that you don't be late. If possible, try to be the first one to arrive. Being on time means that you are interested in meeting that person.

2. **Just be yourself.** You won't be making a good first impression if you will force yourself to impress someone

whom you're meeting for the first time. Just be yourself. Don't pretend to be someone you are not.

3. Present yourself appropriately. To make a good first impression, physical appearance matters. Since the person whom you're meeting for the first time has no idea of who you are or what kind of personality you have, the way you look is the first clue that he or she has on you. But this doesn't mean that you have to look like a celebrity to create a good impression. All you need to is to present yourself appropriately. Presenting yourself appropriately doesn't only include the clothes you'll be wearing but your over-all demeanor as well. So be sure to present yourself appropriately at all times.

4. Always put on a winning smile. There's a saying that goes something like this, "Smile and the world smiles too." So in creating a good first impression, nothing beats a winning smile. Be sure to greet everyone with a genuine smile and surely they will smile back at you.

5. Be confident. It is normal for you to get nervous when meeting somebody for the first time. Sometimes, this nervousness often leads to nervous habits and sweaty palms. So what you need to do is to control your feeling of being nervousness. This can be done by believing in yourself. How can you be nervous if you have confidence within you?

6. Be positive. Having a positive outlook in life is always a good attitude to have. If you have a positive attitude, all the negativity will be blocked. Your positive attitude will show in everything and anything you do. Projecting a positive attitude, even when faced with criticism, always result to a good first impression.

They say that first impressions last. That is true. That is

why it is very crucial that all friendships start on the right foot.

Most of the times, what people think of you the first time they see you stays in their memories for quite a while. And though it is possible that their first impression of you will change once they get to know you more, it is always better that friendships start on a positive way.

But giving a good first impression is only half of the battle because the real challenge is how to maintain it. For example, if people's first impression of you is that you're a responsible person, it is imperative that you be responsible in everything and anything you do, especially when you are with your friends because they expect you to be one.

3

BE INTERESTINGLY FUNNY

So what kind of first impression can be considered a good kind of first impression? Well, it really depends on your personality. As they say, what you see is what you get so just be true to yourself, and hopefully people will learn to accept you for who you really are.

But if there's one thing that can make a good first impression to most people, it is by having an interestingly funny personality. Being interestingly funny means being able to make people around you like you through laughter.

Being interesting and funny are two different personalities. You can have an interesting personality but it doesn't necessarily mean that you can be funny as well and vice-versa.

So being "interestingly funny" requires a lot more than just having the ability to crack a joke or two. You should have a personality that people will be interested in knowing. To be funny, you need to think of yourself as someone who performs for your friends, like how a performer makes his or her audience laugh. In other words, you have to be the life of the group. Also, for you to be "interestingly funny", it is a must that you know yourself first. And this book will teach you what characteristics potential friends will surely find interesting in you.

If you want to be interesting to your friends, here are some ideas that can help you along the way. First thing to know about being interesting is about introducing people to new things. If you want to make friends with people you've met for the first time, it will help if you can introduce them to things that they probably don't know. People will find you interesting if you have the knowledge or information that they would like to have, but don't have yet.

For people to see you as an interesting person, live a fun life as possible. Being interesting is not just about waiting at your house before actually meeting with your friends. Being interesting is about living a fun and exciting life. Try to become the type of person who always has new things to show to everyone. If you are fun to be with, people will surely want to make friends with you.

Another way to be an interesting person is learning to present what you want to say in an engaging manner. Two people can have the same story to say but how they say it differently makes the story more interesting. One can tell the story straight-forward lacking the emotion required to make the story engaging. While the second one can tell the story with enough energy, making the story less boring and more entertaining.

Having an interesting personality also means developing an instinct for things that people would want to hear. This is self-explanatory; nobody cares about things that don't interest them. It is pointless to say something to another person who doesn't seem to care to hear what you want to say. This is why it is important that you know who you're talking to so that you can adjust what you want to say to what he or she would want to hear. For example, if you are trying to start a conversation with someone who likes basketball, don't try to talk about stuff about the solar system. Try to start the conversation by talking about things that has something to do with basketball.

Lastly, being interesting is all about your being unique and different from everyone else. Simple logic dictates that how can you be interesting to others if you have almost the same things to day or to do like the rest of them. Being interesting means that you have something that only you can offer.

4
BE MEMORABLE

Be memorable can mean a lot of things but one clear and simple definition of being memorable is making people miss you whenever you are not around. It is having a kind of persona that sticks to the minds of people you meet.

Friends should not forget you after meeting you for the first time. Giving a good first impression is good, but giving a lasting good impression is better.

One effective way, of making your future friends remember you, is to leave them with a "mark" of your personality. It could be how you talk, how you laugh or how you smile. It has to be something that is distinctly yours - something that will remind them of you all the time.

Always remember that the most important thing to take note when meeting people for the first time is to just be yourself, and not act like somebody else. Don't try to play a role because it will just appear that you're trying so hard to impress.

As the saying goes, "Don't just be yourself. Instead, be the best possible version of yourself." This simply means that for people to remember you, try to show them all the best things about you.

One way of making people not forget you is by getting them to laugh. Try to watch a comedy movie and you can prove to yourself that every time you recall a funny scene in the movie, you can't help but to laugh. This is because happy thoughts are always easier to recall than sad thoughts.

In making friends, if you give them the first impression that you are the type of person who exudes happiness and a jolly personality. For sure, nobody will forget you.

5

LEARN TO LISTEN

Another good trait to have for you to make friends is having the ability to be a good listener. Being a good listener means you are sensitive to the needs and wants of the people you interact with.

Nobody wants to be friends with someone who doesn't know when to stop talking and start listening. Learning to listen is very important for a friendship to prosper because it gives you the opportunity to learn more about your friends.

Being a good listener needs you to have two characteristics. First one is sensitivity while the second one is patience.

A literal definition of sensitivity is being sensitive to things that are happening around you. But in listening, sensitivity is the ability to react appropriately during different situations. Being sensitive means knowing when to listen and when to talk.

For example, if you have a friend who wants to confide to you a problem about his or her love life, you should be sensitive enough to listen to your friend as he or she vents all her disappointments and frustrations. You should not attempt to give advices, unless your friend asks for your advice.

On the other hand, patience, also called forbearing, is being able to endure difficult situations, which means having the ability to persevere when provoked. Simply defined, patience is being able to stay calm and collected even when under stress. When it comes to listening, patience simply means knowing when, what and how to react when faced with different situations.

In making friends, learning to listen is important because it the only way we get to know people. In fact, listening is considered as one of the most important, if not the most important skill that you should have. How well you are in listening will have a great impact on the quality of friendships you will have with people.

Through listening, we can obtain important information about our friends. We can learn things we *should* know about them; both the good and the bad. This information can help us in dealing with our friends during good and bad times.

Another benefit of being a good listener is getting to understand people. If you don't listen to what people will say, there is a chance that you will not understand their personalities altogether.

Listening also results to having a feeling of enjoyment. If you don't get bored listening, it means that you are simply enjoying what you are hearing. Listening to what your friend has to say, no matter how trivial it is, is an integral part of maintaining a healthy and productive friendship.

6

YOUR BODY LANGUAGE

By definition, body language is a form of non-verbal communication. It is a way of expressing what people feel or want to say through their physical behavior.

Body language can be expressed through body posture, facial expressions, hand gestures and eye movements.

Generally-speaking, body language is a sub-conscious behavior by nature making it totally different from another form of non-verbal communication, called sign language, which is an intentional act of communication done by a conscious person.

Body language can provide hints or clues as to the actual state of mind of an individual. It can also give an idea on what the over-all attitude of the person is. Body language can indicate boredom, pleasure and even intoxication. An intoxicated person who says he's sober can't hide the truth about his real condition. Even if he says that he is not intoxicated, the way he talks and walks says otherwise.

Body language is very important in relationships and communication. And although body language is not spoken, it can still disclose many things about one's true feelings to other people and how these people actually reveal how they feel towards you.

Understand that body language is a very important tool in communication that constitutes fifty percent of what people are trying to say with other people. So if you want to know how to communicate effectively using your body, it is just right to know how you can and can't do with your body to say what you want to say.

The important thing to know in body language is determining what kind of messages or signals you are trying to send. Our bodies can be likened to walking advertisements that display our inner feelings and thoughts. So when using body language as a means of communicating with friends, always be sure that you are sending the correct signals. This is very crucial because how your body behaves says a lot about what you want to say or want to do.

Clear examples of body language that you can use to friends are a smile and a hug. Smiling is the simplest yet most effective way of communicating in a non-verbal way. You don't have to say how happy you are seeing a friend or how grateful you are to a good deed that a friend has done for you. A smile is more than enough to say how you really feel. On the other hand, hugs are effective in expressing certain emotions like love and fear. You can hug a person because you want to show how much you love him or her. But on the contrary, a young child who's hugging his or her parent and not letting go simply means that he or she is afraid and only finds comfort with hugging.

When it comes to making friends, body language is important because it gives your friends an idea on how you really feel inside. You may be saying one thing but actually meaning another thing.

For example, if your friends ask your opinion about something and you say you agree just because you don't want your friends to get offended, but deep inside you totally disagree with what they're saying; it will show in your body language that you are actually disagreeing.

You can't hide what you really feel inside because it will show in your body language. So the best thing to do is to say what you feel. No pretensions. This way, anything and everything that you will be saying to people will come from the heart.

7

DO YOUR RESEARCH

All friends know one another. What each friend likes or dislikes. This is important because it will help the friendship workout smoothly.

So if you want to expand your circle of friends, it is a must to research about your potential friends. Research that could include what kind of music they love to listen to, what kind of movies they like to watch or what kind of food they want to eat. Little things that help you understand them better.

Starting a friendship can be easy if you have the right idea on what people like their friends to be. Generally, people love friendly and funny individuals because they are not boring to be with and they bring out certain aspects about their personality that most people don't normally see.

In doing your research, be sure to know the most interesting things about them. These things can jump-start a friendly conversation. Who knows? You might find things that they like that you like as well.

In terms of being able to make people laugh, research is

very important. Just like any comedian, knowing the latest material that can be used as source of a punchline is critical.

If you don't do your research, things might not turn out the way you want them to be. It is like going to war unprepared and not having a clear strategy on how to defeat your enemies.

Research requires knowing what kind of information you need, information that you can use to make a good impression of yourself to people. You don't need to know everything about the people you want to be friends with. All you need are things that can give you an idea of what kind of person he or she is.

8

SOCIAL MEDIA

Social media refers to the creation, sharing and exchanging of ideas and information through virtual social communities and networks. Media used to refer to the three things where people get their information from namely: television, radio and newspaper; collectively known as tri-media.

But due to the advent of modern technology, another source of media called the internet is slowly gaining popularity. But unlike tri-media, the internet is a virtual source of information.

When you say virtual social communities and networks, these refer to social networking sites such as Facebook and Twitter.

These are the kind of sites where you can get to know people who can eventually become your friends. You can also use Facebook to find friends that you have lost contact with - friends from your childhood days to friends that you had during college.

But making friends through social media has both its advantages and disadvantages.

One good advantage of making friends through social media is giving yourself the opportunity to make friends with a lot of people from all over the world. Social media websites like Facebook can be accessed by people anywhere in the world. This gives you the chance to meet people and make friends with them regardless where they are. The potential of making friends through these social media sites is limitless.

But on the other hand, since you only get to interact with your friends once you are online, that's one disadvantage of making friends through social media. The things you get to know about your virtual friends are limited to the information he or she provides on his or her Facebook account.

Making friends using social media is good at a certain level. What's important is getting to know your Facebook friends on a personal level. There should come a time in your friendship that you meet one another in person. Although meeting somebody you've only met online presents safety and security issues, it is important that you meet the person in the flesh if you want your friendship to prosper.

Although it is true that social media can help you make friends, nothing beats going out of your house to meet people that you interact with daily in your life.

9

GET A HOBBY

A hobby, by definition, is an activity that a person does for pleasure on a regular basis. It is something that you can do on your free time such as playing basketball or painting.

But in terms of making friends, getting a hobby isn't just about you and what you like to do for fun. It is more on what kind of hobbies can get do to meet other people. You should find a hobby that involves socializing with others. Don't look for a hobby that you can do all by yourself. Look for an activity that will require you to go out of your house and mingle with people.

Since a hobby is a social activity, interacting with others is inevitable. Find a hobby that gives you the opportunity to know people.

You might be surprise that you can actually find friends in different places like gyms, parks and fast-food chains. The trick is going to places to do things that you genuinely like and from there try to socialize with people who have the same interests as you.

There are many types of hobbies that you can do. Hobbies that a lot of people also love to do.

To give you an idea on what types of hobbies can find you friends, here are some hobbies that you can do:

Collecting

Collecting, as a hobby, includes seeking, getting and keeping things that interests you the most. If you like collecting stamps, you can go to events where you can meet other stamp collectors as well. As the saying goes, "birds of the same feather, flock together." So people who love to collect the same items will likely end up as friends in the future.

Outdoor recreation

Another hobby that you can do where you can meet possible friends is through activities that you do outdoors. Outdoor activities like hiking, fishing and gardening can help you meet friends while enjoying the activity at the same time.

Performing arts

If you love to sing, dance or act. You can join workshops where you can meet other people who love to perform as well.

There a more hobbies out there that you can do besides the ones mentioned above. But take note that in choosing a hobby, the most important thing is to find a hobby that you truly love to do while giving you the best chance to meet as many people possible.

10

COMEDIC DELIVERY

Comedic delivery is the way you deliver a comedic punchline. It requires having the right timing when to deliver the punchline. It has to be at the right moment. Not too early and not too late. A punchline that is not delivered at the right time will not be as funny as intended.

Comedic delivery, also referred to as comic timing, is the use of tempo and rhythm in improving humor. It also involves knowing when to pause to allow your audience to laugh at the joke. Delivery in comedy is important because it definitely has a great impact on the comedic effect of a joke.

Having the perfect comedic delivery can be in-born in nature and can be learned. There are people who are born with the natural talent of being able to deliver a punchline perfectly and effortlessly. One perfect example is Charlie Chaplin whose comedic delivery is flawless. Even during his time when comedy films are without audio, Charlie Chaplin was able to make people laugh with just a flip of his cane and with the way he walked.

You are lucky if you are the kind of individual, who was born with the natural comedic delivery timing. Everything you do or say can easily make your friends laugh, a natural born comedian. Who wouldn't want to be friends with someone who is naturally funny?

In case you are not born with natural talent of delivering punchlines with ease, don't worry because comedic delivery can be learned through constant practice. Watch comedy films and television shows like sitcoms and gags show and try to study how the actors deliver their lines. Sites such as: www.comedycentral.com, www.youtube.com, and www.vimeo.com have plenty.

11

FASHION, PANACHE AND COMEDY

In making friends, these three things should also be considered: fashion, panache and comedy.

Fashion is the common term used to refer to a popular practice or style. Fashion can be associated with so many things such as clothing, make-up and even furniture.

In a nut-shell, fashion is a way of self-expression. They even say that what you wear is a reflection of who you are. If you are the type of person who is very conscious with what kind of clothes you wear, they say that you have a conscious personality as well.

Fashion, in terms of making friends, is important particularly in the getting to know stage of the friendship. It is still part of what kind of impression people will have of you the first time you meet. That is why having a good fashion sense is necessary. You don't have to spend a lot and buy expensive branded clothes to impress. Just make sure that you are comfortable with what you're wearing and everything will be fine.

Panache is defined as the flamboyant confidence of style by a person. In other words, it is being comfortably confident with your self. This is important, especially if you want to make a good first impression because if you lack confidence, it will be hard for you to express yourself. If you can't express yourself to people you want to be your friends, how can they get to know you?

Lastly, comedy is essential if you want to have friends because comedy gives life to the friendship. Comedy adds spice to any relationship. If you are able to make your friends laugh especially during the times when they're sad, you are a good friend to have.

AFTERWORD

Nobody said that making friends is an easy thing to do, especially if you're talking about finding true friendship.

But this book has given you an idea on how you can make friends easily and effortlessly.

All you need to do is to be funny and interesting at the same time. It's also an advantage if you can make people around you laugh because it will be easier for them to like you that way.

Mentioned in this book are key factors that can help you make friends. But to summarize everything that has been said in this book, don't forget to do the following:

- Try to spend more time around people. In other words, socialize.
- Try to join as many organizations or clubs with people who have the same interests as you.
- Try to be a good talker and good listener. You can easily make friends if you know when to open your mouth and when to close it too.
- Try to be yourself all the time. Don't pretend to

be someone you are not. Friend wants their
friends to be real always.

Now that you have an idea on what you need to do in order to make friends, don't just sit there doing nothing!
Go out! Have fun! Enjoy life! Meet new friends!

www.ingramcontent.com/pod-product-compliance
Lightning Source LLC
Chambersburg PA
CBHW070037040426
42333CB00040B/1710